A Pretty Great Life

A Pretty Great Life

Life Lessons and Beauty Secrets
from a Hollywood Makeup Artist

Carolyn Simon

BALBOA.PRESS
A DIVISION OF HAY HOUSE

Balboa Press books may be ordered through booksellers or by contacting:

Balboa Press
A Division of Hay House
1663 Liberty Drive
Bloomington, IN 47403
www.balboapress.com
844-682-1282

Print information available on the last page.

ISBN: 978-1-9822-7825-0 (sc)
ISBN: 978-1-9822-7827-4 (hc)
ISBN: 978-1-9822-7826-7 (e)

Library of Congress Control Number: 2021924830

Balboa Press rev. date: 01/13/2022

The Life

To the pretty.

And the pretty kind.
And the pretty funny.
And the pretty smart.
And the pretty strong.

To help all of you enjoy a pretty great life!

My Path

My genes and experiences make me up.

Ifeoluwa Egbetade   Writer and businessman

How did a French major from Massachusetts end up as a Hollywood makeup artist? It was not a direct path, by any means. This Irish Catholic girl, one of eight children (four boys, four girls), started out as a shy little blonde. At about seven years old, with my crooked teeth, many freckles, and mousy hair cut into a pixie style, I felt more like an ugly duckling. Somehow about that same time though, a strong sense of style began to emerge.

My mom remembers that as a young girl, I refused to wear anything made of polyester. I suppose I just wanted better options. While my sisters weren't allowed to get the cute Mary Jane shoes for school, I asked and was surprisingly permitted to wear them. In sixth grade, when caught wearing nail polish (which was banned at my Catholic school), I was sent home to learn a lesson. My mom somehow held in her laughter until after we left the nun's office.

Life got much better after middle school. Braces came off and my hair grew to my waist; I began to blossom. High school meant lots of friends, both girls and boys, and it was my goal to always look my best.

At home, we had one bathroom for eight school-aged children, and we never knew when the hot water would run out. Not wanting to suffer a cold shower, I would get up earliest. After showering, I faithfully did my makeup in the dusty, dimly-lit mirror by the front door. On days when pressed for time or I just didn't feel like making up my face, fellow students would always ask if I felt sick or was tired. Those remarks helped me to realize the power of makeup.

My initial break in the business of beauty came the summer after high school. I was hired at a high-end hair salon on Newbury Street in Boston, though I had no formal experience. As their in-house makeup artist, I offered clients makeovers to pair with their new hairdos and sold the salon's exclusive products. I quickly learned how to apply makeup on others, especially the mature customers who were the bulk of the salon's clients. It was fun and exciting for me; no two days were ever the same.

While working in the salon was enjoyable, my vision had always been to work for an airline and to travel the world. After Eastern Air Lines posted a local position, I jumped at the opportunity. Initially hired for reservations duty, I was also waitlisted for their flight attendant position. My dreams were beginning to come true.

After several years booking reservations, I was promoted to management and moved south to Miami, Florida. A year later, I became a flight attendant for The Wings of Man. One of the fun parts about starting this job was getting a beauty makeover at a local department store's salon. Their hair stylist helped you to decide if you looked better with bangs or highlights, in short hair or long. The makeup artist looked at your features and did an application to bring out your best assets. It was the first time I had ever had my makeup done by someone else! I left that makeover beaming, excited about my new look which included a berry lipstick and golden highlights in my hair.

Working as a crewmember was so exciting; we got to travel throughout the United States, Canada, and South America. I explored many cities and discovered their restaurants, museums, and culture. Each day meant a different flight crew and new passengers.

Now the question becomes "How did a flight attendant end up as a Hollywood makeup artist?" You've heard the corny expressions "Coffee, tea, or me?" or "Marry me, fly for free" right? Well, that came true in my case. Three years into flying, I met my future husband on a flight from St. Thomas to Miami. Later that fall, I followed him to Los Angeles. Since there was no crew base at LAX, it wasn't possible to continue flying. I transferred back to computer reservations and trained travel agents on the airline's automation system. My wings were officially clipped.

After several years in SoCal, another pivotal moment in my life occurred while doing my cousin-in-law's makeup for her wedding. She radiated beauty naturally, but even more so after a few of my brush strokes with makeup. My husband, a sound mixer in Hollywood, was pleasantly surprised to learn of this skill of mine, one that he had never seen. He suggested pursuing a career in his industry. Thrilled with that idea, I reduced my workload to a part-time clerical position at the airline and enrolled in the best makeup school at the time, Joe Blasco Makeup Center in Hollywood.

Each class was a totally unique experience. I would come home in wildly creative looks: one time bald as an eagle, another time bloodied like a boxer, and yet another covered with feathers and prosthetic pieces for a fantasy creation. Occasionally I would look beautiful too. After six months of training, it seemed fitting that my model for the final would be Sonia, my cousin-in-law who started it all with her wedding. The assignment was to transform her into Betty Boop for my diploma. It was a perfect choice for her facial shape and I recreated the character successfully. I had become a certified makeup artist!

The next part of my makeup career was the toughest: gaining experience. Not quite ready for Hollywood, I started working on American Film Institute (AFI) student projects. My first film was called *Jam the Transmissions*. I highly doubt that anyone beyond the AFI students actually saw it, but working on this film and others was a great way for me to learn the ins and outs of the movie business. It answered questions like: Who does what on set? What the heck is a gaffer? When was it okay for me to step in to make adjustments? How did my work look on the monitors? It taught me a few lessons too, like: Watch out for all those cables and c-stands! And don't eat too much at the craft service tables. Stuffing your face means you are just bored.

All that effort and teamwork paid off when the movie was finally screened. I sat back and admired the end result. The best part? My name rolling by in the film's credits.

Another big step in building my skill was working at a local glamour portrait studio. They were a huge trend in the late eighties and early nineties, where ladies had their makeup done, hair teased, and necklines draped with poufy tulle fabric. Then it was all captured on film. A constant line outside the studio forced me to work quickly and seeing the proofs provided immediate feedback on the quality of my work. These two experiences, along with makeovers for all of my girlfriends, helped build my confidence and speed.

Now that I felt ready, I reached out to a few contacts in the industry. Slowly, I began to build a roster of clients, both personal and production. My skills got better with each gig. While still working part-time for the airline, I taught at a theatre camp over several summers, sharing the excitement of clown, old age, and special effects makeup applications with young students. I volunteered for Girl Scouts of America events like their Cookie Kickoff and anywhere else possible.

As the year 2000 approached and my twenty-year anniversary in the airline industry was upon me, it seemed like the right time to make a change. I quit my job to focus solely on makeup. It truly was a leap of faith, with no turning back. Scary, but oh so exciting!

Now years later, with lots of practice in the industry, I share tips learned along the way. Lessons that have changed my application techniques and also my perspective. Ones that enabled me to grow as a makeup artist, but more importantly, as a person. Continue to read along for a fascinating peek through the eyes of this regular girl working in Tinseltown!

The Pretty

Trendy or Timeless

Beauty, to me, is about being comfortable in your own skin. That, or a kick-ass red lipstick.

Gwyneth Paltrow   Actress and businesswoman

Intimidated by the number of choices available when it comes to makeup? Even as a professional, I sometimes feel that way. Since the makeup industry is part of the fashion world, it sells the latest trends. While being current is definitely fun, the sheer volume of options can be exhausting and expensive.

Consider the almost infinite colors of eyeshadows. You could buy a ton of colors and still feel the pressure to buy the latest Pantone color choice. But should you?

Would you like a pro's advice for buying eyeshadows? Start with brown eyeshadow. Yes, that is correct, brown. It is my go-to shade. Brown is majorly underappreciated; it is extremely versatile. First, there are so many wonderful shades of it: warm, cool, light, medium, or dark. Second, it can look natural for the conservative ladies, as well as super dramatic for the divas in the house. Find the tone that looks great on you and you won't be fooled into buying the latest and greatest new eyeshadow palette. Unless you are a collector and can't live without it. Or if it has lots of browns.

What about lipstick? Did you know that waitresses who wear red lipstick earn more money? It's been proven. Studies have shown that with all else being equal, customers tip more generously those servers who wear a crimson shade on their lips. Other studies report that women who wear red are considered more attractive. Both sound good to me. If a bright and opaque red is too much for you, why not try a sheer formula and see if your income or love life improves? It might make a difference!

Certain styles of makeup transcend times. The sooty kohl eyeliners discovered by early Egyptians continue to be worn today. The current smoky and cut-crease eyeshadow techniques can be traced back to silent film starlets. And the sex kitten look (think Brigitte Bardot) with black cat eye and nude lip remains ever popular with modern women.

Rather than follow the most recent trend of the month, look instead to classic Hollywood stars for inspiration. Are you a Grace Kelly, an Angela Bassett, or an Ariana Grande type? When looking at your favorite medium, take careful notice of celebrities' complete looks including hair, makeup, and wardrobe. Their fashion choices may be similar to those from years past; great looks never go out of style. See if you can find a beauty mentor – someone you resemble – and mimic that person's style. Your beauty icon may change over the years, but it is nice to have a celebrity or personality who you can echo when shopping for clothes, makeup, and even haircuts. My favorite in recent times has been Jennifer Aniston. Who will be yours?

Primer

Beneath the makeup and behind the smile I am just a girl who wishes for the world.

Marilyn Monroe   Actress

If I am a painter, then your skin is my canvas. For my work to look good, it really helps for you to have clear and moisturized skin. Sometimes because of genes or stress, skin can be less than perfect. At times I am asked by clients, "How can I cover my acne?" or "How might I hide these brown spots?" Honestly, you shouldn't have to on a regular basis. If your skin, which is your largest organ, needs medical attention please see a dermatologist. Some things require professional care.

Prepping for makeup generally begins with a primer. Continuing the comparison with painting, priming gets the canvas ready for paint. "It is a crime not to prime," is a mantra for many makeup artists. This step helps even skin tone and smooth its texture. Primer allows makeup to glide on effortlessly and even last longer. It might be something worth trying if you have any of those issues.

For tired or dry eyes: Before you put on any makeup, use a lubricant or liquid tears product specifically made for your need. I keep drops in my kit for exactly these situations. A great cat eye, your favorite eyeshadow, or amazing brows won't pop in the desired way with red or scratchy eyes.

For dark circles under eyes: For a fair complexion, use a peach tone corrector. Darker? Use a deeper orange one. If you don't have either, you can also try red lipstick (but not a long-wearing one nor on a daily basis; this is for emergencies only). Use just enough to neutralize the discoloration. Blend it well, but not so much that it disappears. Then, tap your foundation over the corrector using a patting motion. It really works.

For choosing the best foundation: Most people love how foundation evens the many tones of a face. Look first at your décolletage (neck/chest area) and match your face to the color you find there. Very often, the face is either ruddier (from too much sun) or fairer (from using lots of sunscreen) than the rest of the body. You don't want to look like a head floating on a different colored body. Match the color in natural lighting, not under the fluorescent bulbs of retail stores, to make the best selection. Note: if your foundation tends to rub off around your nose area, then try using an eyelid primer under your foundation around your nose. Just like it keeps your eyeshadow from budging, it can also help your foundation from disappearing.

For flaky lips: Use a lip exfoliant to remove chapped areas. No lipstick is flattering on rough texture. And remember, the best lip look of all is when you smile as you greet someone!

Ageless

Beauty begins the moment you decide to be yourself.

Coco Chanel Fashion designer

Are you feeling the pressure to look young? The media we see ensures most of us do, regardless of age. Twenty-year-olds are already doing Botox injections in an attempt to stall aging. It can be disheartening, but there is hope.

The long-standing basics such as taking good care of your skin, exercising, and eating well are still the most helpful actions you can take. They result in both feeling and looking younger than your age. Of course, just simply accepting aging is the most important action. But there are a few youth enhancing secrets that I would like to share with you.

Something you should incorporate into your routine is wearing sunscreen on your face every day. Use a separate product that is applied under, not in, your foundation, with at least SPF 30. Be sure to include your neck and hands. Though you might not notice it immediately, it consistently helps to slow many of the signs of aging.

Next, please don't over-pluck your brows. Once removed, hair often refuses to grow back where it once was. You will be stuck with barely-there brows. Fuller brows definitely make you look younger. Think of Brooke Shields' or Cara Delevingne's brows. Like eyeshadow colors, brow trends come and go. Don't pay too much attention to the hype. Keep your brows neatly shaped and full.

Wearing a matte texture or too dark of a lipstick color can also age you. Instead, choose a creamy formulation in a color that is light to medium in hue. Opt for one that is vivid and bright if that's more your style. Either will definitely be more flattering.

Like to glow with highlighter? It is one of my favorite ways to show off the best parts of a client's face. It can make you look like you are glowing from within. Keep in mind when incorporating this technique, that mature skin looks better with liquid and cream products. Powder highlighters accentuate texture, so they look best if you don't have any acne scars, wrinkles, or imperfections on the skin surface where applied. And frost or iridescent highlighters are only flattering on clients with exceptional skin.

Liquid eyeliner that is too pronounced or too much of an exact line is not flattering on most women. Instead, use an eye pencil that can be softened or smudged to create a softer look. The goal is more of a shadow than a line. If in doubt, blend it more.

Speaking of more, too much of a good thing (makeup) is best avoided for those wanting to look youthful. Creases in skin become more obvious, and complexions appear dull with too much foundation. I recommend using the sheerest of products that provide coverage without looking like a mask. You might have to touch up your problem areas with a concealer, but don't lay it on thick all over. If you have freckles, I suggest that you let them show.

Straight white teeth are always in style. If you had braces, thank your parents and please continue to wear your retainer. Teeth can shift even many years later. As far as color, too much wine, coffee, or smoking encourages stains on those pearly whites. Over-the-counter whitening products do work to reverse the damage and can bring back your beautiful smile.

What else helps? Limit your use of drinking straws. They are bad for the environment and they also age you by ingraining the dreaded vertical lines around your lips. It will appear as if you have been a lifelong smoker whether or not that's true, and that is not flattering on anyone. The only exception regarding straws would be if you are talent on set, need a sip of something, and don't want to mess up your lipstick. Otherwise, I recommend you ditch straws.

While you can't stay forever young, one thing you can and should do is remain stylish. Take the time to find your own unique look. Incorporate only the colors and trends that work well for you. Chasing youth is not attractive. A quiet sense of confidence, however, very much is.

Noir

I love all the colors mixed together, black.

Brian Elston   Artist

Why is black so popular? Ubiquitous in urban areas like New York, Los Angeles, and locations in between, this noncolor seems to be the most popular choice in apparel essentials, my closet included. Have you ever wondered why?

There are many reasons black is a great option. Black is neutral and works with almost everything else in your wardrobe. Along with navy and gray, it is a cornerstone for building a timeless look. You have a little black dress in your closet, right? That, along with your black jeans and jacket, can be dressed up or down for a variety of different looks. They are extremely versatile, sophisticated, and chic. No one notices if you wear these items again and again, as long as you accessorize them differently.

Another huge factor is the slimming effect of black; who doesn't want that? Black helps us lose a few pounds just by getting dressed. Be sure to choose a matte black fabric, which is more forgiving than something shiny. Layering different textures (like leather, spandex, velvet, or silk) keeps this noncolor from looking boring.

This multi-talented hue can also provide a cool, artistic vibe, a je ne sais quoi. This is perfect for creative types in fields like music, dance, fashion, and art. Remember the black berets of beatnik fame? Maybe you are too young to recall, but they were very hip in the '60s.

Speaking of cool, backstage Hollywood has a legitimate reason for sporting black. Film and television crews wear it so that when they walk on set, they will simply fade into the dimly-lit background. Similarly, theatre staff often wear black in an effort to blend in with dark curtains during production breaks.

The beauty industry follows this trend too, but for totally different reasons. Hairdressers sport black clothing, capes, smocks, and aprons to keep dirt and chemicals from staining. It definitely makes things easier on laundry days. Makeup artists also don ebony. Their excuse? Wearing other colors would reflect light and potentially alter their client's skin tone. This could negatively affect the color choices made during an application. What might look great in one light might be totally wrong in another. Artists in retail stores who sell makeup usually wear black. They are hoping that you will notice their makeup rather than their wardrobe and buy more products. And we usually do!

Pop of Color

I'm crazy for color. Color embraces you. It wakes you up and keeps you present.

Tracy Reese   Fashion designer

While all this black looks pretty cool, if you prefer instead to stand out from the crowd, simply add a pop of color to your somber wardrobe. An actress friend regularly wears red when an event calls for black tie. You absolutely cannot miss her at the party.

A thespian colleague shared her favorite auditioning tip: if you are wearing the required black attire, be sure to add a flower in your hair, a colorful hat, or a bold signature necklace. It ensures that later when they are deciding on talent, you will have worn something memorable. "Yes, let's cast the girl with the daisy tucked behind her ear" hopefully would be heard that night. It could also be helpful if interviewing for a position in the beauty field. You would stand out from the crowd of applicants, perhaps, with your unusual jewelry.

Your signature pop of color choice might be a ruby-red lipstick or a classic handbag in an unusual hue, or even a pair of vivid ballet flats that show off your personality. Please, however, keep balance in mind. If you happen to have deep or dark pigment in your hair, skin, or eyes, then the color you choose should be bright or deep as well. But if you are fair and light, a subtler color like mauve or pale blue might be more appropriate. Just keep trying things until you find the item or color that feels right and works for you. A pop of color is the perfect way to express your personality while still fitting in. And it can be a great conversation starter.

Or, go full-on with color. My oldest sister is a teal and purple girl. Open her closet and everything totally matches. She might wear a little bit of black on her bottom half, but finds that bright colors near her face accentuate her best features.

I periodically teach a Color Analysis course and drape various colors of fabric swatches to help determine if students are warm/cool and light/dark. It is fascinating to watch how someone's face does indeed light up with the right color. It's helpful to note that some tones are universally flattering, such as purple, navy, and teal.

Want to know one of the most important color choice items in your wardrobe? Ironically, it's your bathrobe. You sport it with absolutely no makeup, often while tired or pale. Be sure to choose a flattering color; it should look great on au naturel you. For similar reasons, sheets and comforters on your bed are also very important color choices.

When recalling the fabulous dresses from Hollywood's biggest nights, I generally remember the colorful ones. I can vividly recollect Nicole Kidman's chartreuse silk look and Gwyneth's pink satin ball gown for her *Shakespeare in Love* win. Do you remember Michelle Williams in her buttercup-yellow number or Halle's beautiful floral gown that she wore for receiving her honor? And Zendaya's emerald green corset dress for the Emmy Awards was absolutely stunning! The right color on someone is memorable. Don't be afraid to add a splash to your wardrobe and you, too, will be unforgettable.

Learn from Others

I am still learning.

Michelangelo Renaissance artist, at age 87

As an instructor and professional artist, I understand just how important it is to be in a constant state of learning. Even after twenty years in the makeup business, I remain an inquisitive student. While I gain knowledge from my pro artist courses, YouTube, and makeup books, I also learn from clients and even my makeup students.

When putting a product such as gel or pomade in someone's hair, always begin from the back of the head. This way, if you put too much in your hands, you won't mess up the most important part – the front of the hair. Thank you, celebrity client.

Want to curl your lashes but don't have an eyelash curler? Head to your kitchen and pull out a spoon. There is a bit of a learning curve, but this method is very similar to the way that one uses scissors to curl a ribbon. Women in some of the smaller villages of Mexico have passed down this skill from generation to generation. Thank you, student from Mexico.

Need to contour someone with very dark skin when every sculpting product in your kit is too light? Try a matte black eyeshadow instead. I learned this from a daytime talk show professional; it totally works! Thank you, television makeup artist.

Love or need waterproof mascara, but dislike how difficult it is to remove? A tip I learned is to apply a first coat of regular mascara and then make the second one waterproof. It seems that having that first regular layer makes removal a bit easier than if all waterproof. Thank you, beauty influencer.

Speaking of mascara, do you know what some dancers and actors did to enhance lashes before mascara was invented? I watched in awe as a former theatrical performer, the mother of one of my brides, melted black wax and applied it onto her lashes. (Readers, do not try this at home.) She then separated any clumps with a fine sewing needle. Amazing, but I am so glad we have mascara today. Be very careful and thank you, Sonia's mom.

Have you heard about the E3 contouring trick? The right half of a client's face gets the E: start in the upper forehead, come around under the cheekbone, and then follow the jaw line with the contour product. The left side gets the shape of a 3: the same movement and placement, just the other side of the face. Thank you, YouTube artist.

Red lipstick is always popular with women, but what about for men? When an international male model asked me to apply a very sheer layer of deep red to his lips, I was skeptical. Yet somehow, it made him look healthier and more attractive. Thank you, Handsome.

I especially love a tip l learned from an Emmy-winning makeup artist. After his initial application of foundation with a dual-fiber brush, he follows up with a clean brush to buff out the model's just- applied foundation. This second brush removes unnecessary product and reveals skin that looks flawless, almost airbrushed. I now incorporate this technique in all of my applications. Try it in your routine, I think you will really like the effect. Thank you, pro artist.

Lessons come from everyone. Are you curious and open to learning?

pretty

adjective

The person reading this now.

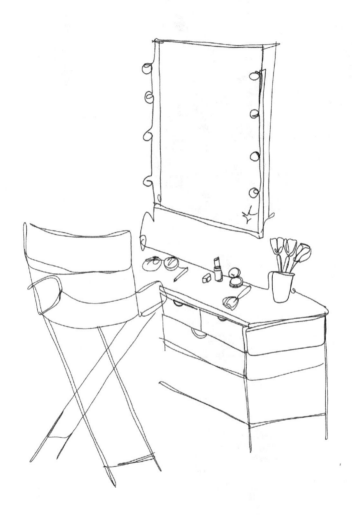

The Artist's Lessons

Homework

The more you do your homework, the more you're free to be intuitive. But you've got to put the work in.

Edward Norton   Actor

The night before a shoot, after receiving my call sheet with the names of talent, I look on IMDB or Wikipedia to learn a little more about them. I seek out photos, read biographies, and educate myself on their repertoire of projects. This research is not necessarily to find topics to discuss with them, but more for things best not said. And it helps to see their approximate complexion type, facial hair, or if they are balding, so that I am better prepped for the job of doing their makeup application the next day. I like to be prepared.

One time, I didn't do my research. I was working with a famous actor and was already familiar with his big projects, love affairs, siblings, appearance – everything I believed I needed to know. But I was mistaken. After the shoot when I looked him up online, I discovered that his middle name was my maiden name. His mother (probably the source of his middle name) was from Boston, my hometown. We might actually be related! Not that I would have even brought it up, because I usually just listen. But still, I potentially missed a golden opportunity. I will probably never know if we are second cousins. But that re-emphasized the importance of doing my due diligence. I vowed from that day forward to do it each and every time.

When it comes to private clients or brides, my homework is simply asking them to share selfies or images of looks they are hoping to recreate. Since I will be meeting them bare-faced, this is very helpful for everyone. It allows me to better understand their makeup goals.

What about you? If you are an aspiring artist, be sure to test products, watch videos, take classes, investigate social media, and ask questions. Not an artist? Explore within your field. No knowledge is ever wasted. Do you do your homework?

Preparation

I will prepare and some day my chance will come.

Abraham Lincoln   American president

Besides makeup, what else helps me do my job? Plenty of things. Yes, my paint and powder supplies are critical for getting most things done, but more often than not, it is the non-makeup items in my kit that save the day. Here are just a few examples:

- **Snacks**: Because you never quite know when the next meal will be coming.
- **Mints**: After your aromatic lunch, clients will appreciate fresh breath.
- **Duct tape**: For removing lint from jackets and sweaters when you can't find the lint roller.
- **Lens cleaner**: Clients love to have their eyeglasses polished and refreshed.
- **Tide to Go Instant Stain Remover Pen and a blow dryer**: For when talent had a flat tire en route and got grease on the front of his favorite (and only) shirt. The Tide Pen successfully cleaned the stain and then my trusty blow dryer quickly eliminated all remaining moisture. Shirt looked as good as new and the interview went off flawlessly.
- **Flashlight**: Ever work in extremely low light conditions or try to clean and pack up in the dark? That has been my situation

on occasion. Petite illuminators that you can hold in your mouth work. A headlamp would be better. You need both hands available to clean up swiftly, so your cell phone's flashlight isn't always the best option.

- **Aspirin, tampons, sunscreen and Band-Aids**: First aid items are priceless to have. Often you will feel like a mom or nurse on set.

While every day is different, it seems that wedding days require the most non-makeup essentials. These items are very frequently requested:

- **Scissors**: For loose threads and tags on dresses.
- **Nail files and clippers**: To smooth out snags or snip a broken nail.
- **Bobby pins**: For hair accessories that won't stay put.
- **Sewing kit, safety pins, and white duct tape**: For securing the bride into her strapless dress when the zipper didn't work, moments before the ceremony. Yes, that really happened and we came to the rescue.

While you cannot predict the future, you can try to anticipate needs and be more prepared. What extras can you add to your bag of tricks to make things go more smoothly?

On Time

Better three hours too soon than one minute too late.

William Shakespeare   Playwright

For those of you unfamiliar with the L.A./Hollywood metropolis, life there revolves around the automobile. And since there are just too many cars for the space on freeways, traffic congestion is a way of life.

When talking about distance to a location, we never mention miles; we refer instead to travel time. We live in fear of sig-alerts (road closures). And traffic applications like Waze are mandatory protocol.

Once, when I traveled to a shoot at the Beverly Hills Civic Center, what should have been an easy forty-five minute drive from Pasadena turned into a two hour prayer vigil. Luckily, I had allowed extra time for a cup of coffee, but used that time instead for sweating bullets as I crawled up the steep canyon road with no alternative options.

An especially precarious predicament occurred one Academy Award evening. The studio had booked me to provide makeup services for the wife of a nominee. Little information was provided up front; I was told the name of the husband and the location at the Four Seasons Hotel, Beverly Hills. As usual, I arrived with lots of extra time and sat in the lobby until my designated call time. I inquired of the lobby receptionist for the room number and the attendant replied, "No one by that name is registered here." Imagine my shock. The guest's first name was something like Brandon or Brendon, one with lots of very similar variations. Perhaps he was registered under a fictitious name? Feeling sorry for me, the receptionist informed me that there was indeed another Four Seasons Hotel in Beverly Hills. This other property was better known as the Beverly Wilshire Hotel (of *Pretty Woman* fame) but privately it too was a Four Seasons location.

Having earlier valeted my car, it was now very deep in the garage and there was insufficient time to get it out. I was going to be late! I summoned Uber and shuttled to the other property, which luckily was only one mile away. Still, there was a lot of traffic, it being L.A. Upon arrival, lobby staff once again informed me that no guest by that name was registered at the property. Panicked, I tried to reach the studio contact who booked me. After a few attempts, I finally spoke to her and learned that the talent was indeed at the original property. I called Uber again and raced back to the first property's front desk, where I found a different staff person this time. When I said the name of my contact, I was given the room number. Whew! And I was only five minutes late. I never said a word to the couple about the confusion; she was ready on time and looked beautiful. That was an awards night and a lesson that I will never, ever forget.

As a former flight attendant, I heard lots of talk about "on-time performance." If he or she was only one minute late for a trip, a crew member would be removed from the assignment. No excuses were accepted. So today, I consider myself fortunate; allowing extra time is deeply ingrained in my DNA. It has saved my job and my sanity on many occasions.

Do you allow extra time for the unexpected? How might things change for you if you did?

Adaptability

You have to be very nimble and very open minded. Your success is going to be very dependent on how you adapt.

Jeremy Stoppelman   CEO and co-founder of Yelp

I often find myself wondering, "What will today be like?" Working freelance, I might have little or no advance information about the talent. I must be extremely flexible kit-wise and prepared for anyone, from the fairest, darkest, warmest, and coolest of skin tones to everyone in between. I may need to mix colors in search of the perfect foundation match if I don't have it. Being creative and thinking on my feet are necessary skills to survive and thrive.

Locations also vary from day to day. I could find myself at a celeb's palatial home or in a dusty, dingy old theatre. I bring a towel or mat to place my makeup upon for either situation. I know a fellow makeup artist who was sued after her brush cleaner spilled on a client's very expensive coffee table. Accidents happen.

Regularly editing my kit is also necessary. I swap out older products when they expire and new ones are required. No funny-smelling or unsafe products for me. Creams and liquids are tossed frequently since they have a short usage span. They need to be used hygienically on palettes when applied on someone other than you. Powders, while they last a little longer, should be sprayed with isopropyl alcohol before or after each client to keep bacteria from developing. Be sure to use new or clean brushes to avoid the spread of germs on professional jobs. And remember to wash your personal brushes. You would be unpleasantly surprised to learn what can collect in your makeup bag.

Sometimes products are eliminated simply by preference. For example, I used to carry brown mascara but noticed that I never used it. Everyone seemed to want black on their lashes, even the fairest of blondes. And individual lashes? I find putting on a full strip of lashes is not only quicker to apply, but I can also cut them into partials for a more minimal look if desired. No need to carry them all.

Another way I stay versatile? My cases. Along with my main Zuca case (rolling storage for supplies), I bring a small set bag and change contents daily depending on my expected schedule. This enables me to better meet the needs of clients that day.

My working locations might be across fields, at beaches, or in historic buildings with no elevators. One shoot was at a famous writer/artist's residence. Or I should say, residences. He had three houses in a row in Beverly Hills: one he lived in, another was his office, and the third was his artist's studio. No matter the location, I bring along only what I can carry, and I wear comfortable, stylish shoes. Very little sitting takes place as a makeup artist.

Adaptability relating to products, bags, locations, shoes, and most importantly, me, helps to ensure success in this industry. In work and in life, it pays to be nimble. How are you doing in this area of your life? Are there things that you could do to improve your success?

Your Niche

You gotta keep trying to find your niche and trying to fit into whatever slot that's left for you or to make one of your own.

Dolly Parton   Singer, songwriter, and actress

What is your specialty or what do you do well?

The old saying, "Jack of all trades, master of none," is one that applies in the makeup industry as well as every other field. Like most makeup artists starting out, I wanted to do it all: film, theatre, bridal, and special effects. It proved very helpful to get experience in many different genres before I narrowed it down to the medium I truly preferred.

I strive to stay skilled in all areas by taking different classes, volunteering, and stretching my limits. But my specialty and most of my bookings are for "clean beauty." It is a makeup application that enhances the client's features without trying to significantly change them. It doesn't mean only a few products, however. Some clean beauty applications can involve up to one hundred items. But the ultimate look is not about noticing the makeup as you might in a Revlon ad; instead, the goal is for you to see that the talent looks their best on screen or in a photo.

Individuals responsible for hiring want to know that you are an expert in the skills they seek. Think about those at the top of the beauty industry. Did Bobbi Brown, the famous makeup icon, do hair? What about hair stylist Vidal Sassoon – did he apply makeup? As they must have honed their skills and narrowed their preferences during their careers, you too would benefit in developing an area of expertise.

If you are a super talented rockabilly makeup artist for print or one who loves doing destination bridal bookings, I recommend that you specialize in that particular niche. Or if you prefer to keep all your options open, simply give the appearance of specialization. Curate separate business cards, collateral material, website pages, and unique portfolios for specific interests. Later, when a prospective client requests information about a select type of service, you can provide them with your customized marketing material for that specific area. Doesn't that make perfect sense?

A former student of mine absolutely loved doing werewolf makeup. It was totally her passion. Her business cards listed that as a specialty and her website had photos and information about this type of makeup application. Do you know how many big producers have contacted her by phone or sent inquiries regarding her services? Quite a few. Why? Simply because they found her when they Googled "werewolf makeup." She might not have had a ton of experience, but she was skilled and knew her passion. So be a detective and find your werewolf makeup. Have you discovered your niche?

Not Too Much

A little bit of powder and a little bit of paint make a woman look like what she ain't.

Unknown

Before versus after makeup images – they are amazing, right? If you are a fan, you know just how transformative makeup can be. Highlighting, contouring, and concealing are a few ways to change the facial shape and correct flaws. Magazines love to do their obligatory "Stars Without Makeup" editions showing celebrities au naturel rather than all dolled up. It helps average people feel a little better, or at least not as bad, about themselves.

Most people are excited to see my workstation well-stocked with a wide variety of products. They can't wait for their transformation to begin. However, there are many others for whom this can be a bit daunting. They may be thinking to themselves, "Am I really that bad? Do I need so much stuff to look good? Will I become a cake face?" Aware of the power of first impressions, I often put out just the basics (I can always add items later if needed) to be sure that I don't overwhelm clients. This is especially true when I work with behind-the-scenes people like writers and directors. Celebrities typically expect the whole shebang.

I tend to apply just enough products to have talent feel beautiful or handsome or simply spoiled. That way, when they are on camera, they possess just the right amount of confidence. Some steps might even seem a little bit like *The Emperor's New Clothes*. For example, when I buff the skin after foundation with a second brush that has absolutely no product. This action has merit; it removes excess product and gives the complexion a glow.

When doing makeup events involving seniors, I almost feel that their post-application sense of beauty stems from something more special than any makeup at all. Simply having a tender interaction helps them feel appreciated. Touch alone is a very powerful force.

Are you heavy-handed with products? Could less actually be more?

Like a Kid

When you think like a child your imagination is free and anything is possible.

Criss Angel Magician and illusionist

What would you do differently if you knew you couldn't fail?

I had some experience with this very topic years ago while teaching at a children's summer camp. The youth participated in art, theatre, and makeup classes each day. The age range of the students was five to twelve years old. I was skeptical that the youngest age group would have the motor skills necessary to complete the makeup exercises. Was I wrong!

The youngest students watched my makeup demonstrations and then, without any hint of hesitation, replicated the details of the work that I had just shown them. They had absolutely no fear of failure, and as a result, usually did an amazing job even on my toughest assignments. Clown, old age, fantasy, cuts and bruises makeup, you name it. I was shocked and quite impressed by their undaunted belief in themselves.

Children are naturally very playful and imaginative. They don't get bogged down with what isn't possible and therefore have endless options. Besides excelling at copying my demonstrations, when the class topics required creativity, my youngest students showed great skill in those challenges as well. They didn't care if you couldn't imagine a rainbow unicorn scarecrow – they did, and found a way to bring it to life. No limits are a good thing!

Apparently as we age, our inner critic along with peer pressure negatively affects our performance abilities. When faced with what seems like a daunting situation, have no limits or fear. What should you do? Pretend that you are a kid and just go for it. How would that change your attitude and your life?

Others First

If you live your life as if everything is about you... you will be left with just that. Just you.

Unknown

Want to make the best impression? Put others first when they are in your presence.

As a makeup artist on set, I imagine myself as the host at my location and the talent as my guest. Their comfort is my ultimate goal. Do they need water or coffee? Do they have a spot to put their purse? Do they need some privacy for a phone call? I am always looking for ways to be of service and to be gracious. After all, it is because of them that I am working.

My own attire, makeup, or demeanor should not attract too much attention. Polished, respectful, clean and neat? Absolutely. But not flashy. It is never polite to upstage the talent; they are the stars.

The makeup application I provide on a project is usually not even my choice of style. Depending on the type of shoot the talent, producer, or perhaps even the photographer makes the decision. While I may have the opportunity to suggest things, a conservative non-makeup wearing client may not want to accept those suggestions.

False lashes, for example, might enhance their overall look, but talent can and often does refuse them.

I recall pleading with a female writer to wear at least a touch of lipstick. I diplomatically explained that since she was on camera with extremely bright lights, she would benefit from a bit of color. Thankfully, she agreed, and everyone was happy with the result. Remember this is their show, not yours or mine. How do you treat others in your life? Could just changing your approach and putting others' needs first make a difference?

Team Player

The main ingredient of stardom is the rest of the team.

John Wooden   Basketball coach

Do you have a group of people who support you? Are you a team player?

I enjoy the camaraderie of being part of a crew. There are usually many players on a shoot, including the cameraman, sound mixer, hair stylist, and makeup artist. We are all there to make the talent look and sound good. Spending long days together, we become like family. It always helps when everyone does their best and gets along. The days are not so mundane when you are with people you like who support each other in a common goal.

One big film company I work with commonly employs a pair of producers for their projects rather than a single person for the role. I believe that having two makes for a better end result. This group's great success reinforces that notion. Each producer has an equal partner on the project, someone who may or may not have similar strengths, viewpoints, and even personality traits in common. Imagine knowing that you have someone to lean on when you are exhausted or someone to fill in when you are not available. Filming with these pairs has always been a very positive experience. This concept really seems to work.

As a makeup artist for weddings, the bridal party and extended family can be large. My last wedding involved eighteen women. Along with the bride, there were fourteen bridesmaids, two mothers (bride's and groom's), and one grandmother. It was impossible for me to do that many clients by myself in the time allowed, so I drafted two fellow makeup artists to assist. These are artists that I enjoy working alongside and we often bounce ideas and jobs off one another. They have become good friends in the process.

Sacrificing your needs for the overall benefit of the team definitely helps all to succeed. Whether for work or for life, friends are the icing on the cake. Have you found your tribe?

The Little Things

Details create the big picture.

Sanford I. Weill   Banker, financier, and philanthropist

Just before the camera rolls, the assistant director will often shout, "Last looks!" This is the time for the hair, makeup, and wardrobe crew to step in and make any final small adjustments to talent that they see needed. Besides the overall framing of the shot, details are equally important. Now that most homes have mega-sized television screens, everything is magnified and in high definition. Contour well blended? Under eye darkness sufficiently corrected? Brows even? So much to consider.

What might not seem obvious to the average viewer must be very evident to trained eyes. I often need to apply makeup to a person's ears, neck, or legs to match their face. You would be amazed how often they are completely different tones. And if full length is being shown, I am literally reaching up under many of my clients' dresses to ensure their pale legs match the rest of their bodies. Once I even had to color correct a weekend golfer's gloved hand to match his ungloved tanned one for an interview. A client has even requested a deeper body makeup color on her arms to look more fit on camera.

If a green screen background is involved in the shoot so that video can be added later, flyaway hairs need to be tucked into place. A smooth and uniform hair outline is critical for post-production.

Continuity is also an important element to consider. If in the first part of an interview, the bottom button of the suit coat jacket was left undone, it must remain exactly the same way throughout the shoot.

When I first meet a client, I become somewhat of a detective. Are they tall or small? Light, medium, or dark complexion? Is their personality outgoing or shy? What about their style? Is it sporty, classic, or feminine? I take in everything, from details to the big picture. Why?

A person is not just their face. Their makeup should reflect and harmonize with their complete look, even if only seen from the shoulders up. An introvert typically is not comfortable in red lipstick even if the color works on them. And soft muted colors would look totally drab on a dramatic beauty.

When two people are in a scene together, I consider how they look as a pair. If she is super dark and he is extremely fair, I might slightly lighten her makeup and darken his so they are not on totally opposite ends of the spectrum. And in pretty much every situation, sweat and shine are not your talent's (or your) friends.

Speaking of sweat and shine, I remember hearing the story of the 1960 Kennedy/Nixon Presidential debate. John F. Kennedy had hired a makeup artist for the event and he looked tan and confident. Richard Nixon, on the other hand, chose not to use a makeup artist. He was sweating profusely under the stage lights, and thus appeared to viewers as anxious or less than truthful. Television audiences overall believed it was Kennedy who won the debate, while those who only listened on the radio overwhelmingly thought Nixon was the victor. Kennedy ultimately won the election and since then, politicians everywhere began using makeup for their big events, televised or not.

Notice everything. Small things can have a huge impact on the big picture. Do you notice the little details?

Nothing

Doing nothing is really heavy work.

Oscar Wilde   Poet and playwright

Once in a blue moon, I have been booked for a shoot only to have the talent decide they don't want makeup that day. Most times it has been situations involving men (such as a few of my lifelong crushes and the most awarded person in Hollywood), but there have been a few women too. Once, a very well-known female celebrity refused makeup three days in a row; she was doing voiceover work and didn't feel makeup was necessary while recording. No problem for me. The rest of the crew, however, was probably a bit jealous; I was getting paid without even lifting a brush. One even wisecracked, "Your best work ever, Carolyn!" On the fourth day, when I did indeed finally get to glamour up her face, it was a glorious experience.

New makeup students often want to do every single step on every single person, but they also need to develop the ability to discern when it might actually be more appropriate to skip a step or put down their brush. Big forehead, chin, or nose? Omit highlighting those areas. Perfect brows already? Don't mess with them; brows shouldn't enter a room before the person does. Restraint is a very valuable skill to acquire.

On a recent shoot, I complimented talent on her hair and she cheerfully replied, "I hardly ever wash it." Later that same day, I mentioned how lovely another person's skin was and she chimed in with, "I rarely wash it." The lesson here? When it comes to one's strands and pores, do almost nothing!

Little or no action might be the best option at times in life, too. It may be necessary to sit back and just observe for a while. Try not to fight it. Be confident enough to know that reflective time can spawn new ideas, creativity, and even better decisions. If we push ourselves to be busy every single second, we don't really listen to what our heads or hearts are telling us. Are you receptive in the quiet moments?

Bad Days

Pour yourself a drink, put on some lipstick, and pull yourself together.

Elizabeth Taylor   Actress and humanitarian

Are my clients nice? Absolutely. After all, I am their ally, there to help them look their best. Every once in a while, however, someone just might be having a bad day and decide to take it out on everyone on set, including me. It happens.

I vividly recall the day I got booked to work with one of my all-time favorite man crushes. He was a total heartthrob actor and director. Handsome. Did I say handsome? I arrived on set and instead found a grumpy middle-aged man with my heartthrob's name instead of the charismatic guy I remembered seeing on the big screen. Wow. What a letdown. Yet because I had done my homework, I knew he was remarried to a much younger woman and they had several very young children at home. Starting all over, coupled with severe lack of sleep, might do that to anyone. So while I was disappointed, I didn't let it show. I tried to make his time in my makeup chair the most relaxing part of his day. Remember, it's not about you.

A similar incident involved a popular comedian. Both times I worked with him he was just plain rude. Ready to pick a fight with anyone and everyone on set. From what I understand, many comedians have dark sides to their personalities and humor is their coping mechanism.

That must have been this man's case. I recently heard that he is on a new series and I pray for the crew working on it. But here again, maybe he was just experiencing a tough stage in his life when we met and he's doing better now. I only wish him success and peace!

I have worked with people in the middle of cancer treatments, celebrities just split from their spouses, those who have front-page tabloid stories being published, executives on the brink of being fired, and mothers of brides with severe OCD. They are all flawed humans just like you and me. They have good days and bad days. Bringing a little sunshine to theirs is the least I can do. What do you do when you need to cheer someone else or yourself up?

Your Words

Your beliefs become your thoughts, your thoughts become your words, your words become your actions, your actions become your habits, your habits become your values, your values become your destiny.

Mahatma Gandhi   Indian lawyer and social activist

Have you ever heard the phrase, "Worrying is like praying for what you don't want?" It really is true. Others feel your vibration, especially when you are up close and personal as their makeup artist. I try to remain calm and positive, regardless of the circumstances around me. No one wants to be with a Debbie Downer. Smiling always helps to lighten the mood.

I like to compliment my clients on at least one of their features. Even if they are not particularly glamorous, each person, male or female, has some aspect – be it eyes, lashes, lips, skin, brows, something – that is attractive. I scan for it and am very sincere when I compliment them. I am being genuine. Star or not, we all like to hear nice things.

In case you didn't realize, a compliment such as "I like your eyeshadow," is not really a compliment. In my opinion, that type of statement is more likely interpreted as "Your eyeshadow would look great on me." A real compliment has nothing to do with the person giving it. "You look great" or "Look at you!" is far more flattering to someone than discussing a specific makeup product or clothing item.

While working alongside another artist, I noticed that as she was applying makeup to her client, she would say things out loud to herself such as "Yes, that's good," or "I like that." I found her technique to be absolutely brilliant. As her client, you don't even need to look in a mirror. You already know you look beautiful!

Compare that to my new students saying "Oops" and "Oh no!" and you soon realize the power of your words. Are you choosing them carefully?

Yes

Success is not a straight line, it's much more of a dance and being open to possibilities.

Arianna Huffington   Author and businesswoman

Though it might appear to be, life is far from linear. Rather, it is mostly circuitous and unpredictable. Being open to new opportunities may offer exciting experiences beyond your wildest imagination. When in doubt, simply say "Yes!"

Starting out as a new makeup artist, I needed to learn many new things beyond the basics taught in makeup school. Apply wigs for a commercial? Sure, I can do it. I researched on the Internet, asked friends who wore wigs, and read whatever I could find on the topic. It was a great success. Beach waves for a popular female celebrity? Of course! She didn't know that I had little experience with that particular style. I practiced a few days before on my own long hair and decided to fake it until I could make it.

Once I was scheduled to meet the Wedding Coordinator at a local church to deliver my business cards. Upon arrival, their receptionist informed me that the Wedding Coordinator was no longer employed there. Her boss then proceeded to ask me if I would be interested in becoming their new Wedding Coordinator. Selling more than one thousand beautiful weddings in that role proved to be an amazing honor that I might have missed, had not been open to listening and saying "Yes."

Through my Girl Scout of America volunteering experiences, I met many local families. When a dad came home from work one day asking his wife if she knew any makeup artists for an open position at his client's college, who do you think she recommended? You guessed it: me. And even though I had never taught Makeup Artistry, I applied for the position. What was there to lose? Now I teach at three colleges.

One never knows where opportunities will present themselves. Are you on the lookout and open to them?

Choices

You can do anything, but not everything.

David Allen   Author and productivity consultant

How much time should a good makeup application take? Forty-five minutes to one hour? Yes, in a perfect world those time frames would be the ideal minimum. However, the reality on set is that time equals money. The crew does not want to wait on makeup.

An airline term often used on set is ETA, estimated time of arrival. One might be asked, "What is your ETA?" In this scenario it translates to, "When will talent be ready?" As an artist, you need to build up your speed so that you can work quickly and efficiently and deliver well-groomed talent promptly.

Knowing I need to work quickly on certain shoots, I try to make makeup choices that will give me the best bang for my buck. Do they have a big nose? Contour it. Gorgeous skin? Be sure to highlight it. No brows? Give them some. An executive might be giving twenty minutes of his extremely busy schedule for the interview and I need to be certain they look their best within the confines of the time allotted.

On a personal level, think about those mornings when you oversleep. If you only had ten minutes to get ready and look presentable to the world, what makeup choices would you make? Would it be mascara to open your eyes? Or a bold lipstick to bring attention to your smile?

Are you familiar with the quality triangle? It is a commonly referenced diagram (not my creation) which demonstrates priorities and choices. This triangle can be used for different types of businesses, not simply for makeup services. The premise is that you may only choose two of the three corners:

The Quality Triangle
(pick two)

Fast

Good   Cheap

So if it is cheap and fast, it won't be good. Cheap and good? Not fast. The one we all strive for? Fast and good, which merits you, the provider of services, the highest salary since it won't be cheap!

Here is a fun personal beauty version:

The Beauty Triangle
(pick two)

Makeup

Hair   Wardrobe

So if your makeup and hair are on point, perhaps your wardrobe is lacking. Hair and wardrobe? Not much time for makeup. You get the idea!

And lastly, an amusing one about dating:

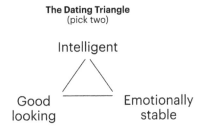

The Dating Triangle
(pick two)

Intelligent

Good looking — Emotionally stable

But seriously, let's get back to choices. If I had limited time and had to pick only one area to focus on for a makeup application, it would be to ensure that my client's skin looked great. No dark shadows, no uneven tones, etc.

The ultimate lesson here? Always take good care of your skin so that looking your best will be easy. Do you agree?

Your Lane

Don't believe the hype. I don't care how many number ones you have at the box office. I don't care how much they say you're great, don't believe it. Just stay in your lane and do what you're supposed to do.

Tyler Perry   Actor, writer, and producer

There are many players on a production crew, and their roles are often quite specific. Without boring you by listing each one of them, I will simply mention those that relate to the talent's look on set. They are the hair, wardrobe, and makeup crew members. On larger shoots, all three specialties have someone responsible. On smaller productions, it might be that no one is covering any of them.

As a makeup artist, I am strictly responsible for the complexion and makeup of talent. It can be as basic as just a touch of anti-shine product or the full deal from primer to false eyelashes. If there happens to be a separate stylist or hair person designated on the job, I must never ever touch the clothing or hair of talent. It is truly off-limits.

Working as a member of a team, I am aware to never step on another crew member's toes. But there are other times when I am the only person on set in the image area and I tuck in collars, clip the backs of shirts, remove lint, and curl hair. Want to keep friends on set? Definitely stay in your own lane.

This can also get tricky in the world of runway and fashion shows where one finds so many models and makeup artists. It is a fun but crazy atmosphere. A word of advice relating to this chaos: be sure not to ever touch another artist's work. If a model asks you to do so, simply refuse. Direct them back to their original artist to make adjustments. It is never appropriate for you to alter someone else's artistic creation.

The acronym MYOB was very popular when I was growing up. It stands for Mind Your Own Business, and it still very much applies all these years later. It is a valuable key to success. Do you keep in your own lane and stay on track?

Perspective

Above all else, I want to see things differently.

Lesson 28, A Course in Miracles

Where is the best place to do your makeup? Without a doubt, it is in natural lighting. Cozy up next to a window during the daytime if you want to be sure the colors and application look just right. While those conditions may seem somewhat harsh, if the makeup appears flawless there it will perform well anywhere.

Since daylight is not always an option, when painting faces, I try to consider the location where the makeup will ultimately be viewed. Is it for a beach or a candlelit wedding? Or on a production stage flooded with lights? The look could and usually should vary, depending on the venue. More lights mean more intense coloring, but not necessarily more product.

On-set monitors help determine if I need to tweak the makeup application once the talent has settled into the shot. The lighting of the makeup area could have been quite different from the tones on set. I watch the monitors once rolling begins to keep an eye out for any new changes such as sweating or oxidation of foundation, things that might require my intervention.

My vision and that of my clients can at times be very different. That is why I often present colors and ask if those particular hues are pleasing to them. If we are not at a makeup station, I provide a mirror so the client may check her reflection periodically. My version of her brows might be totally different than what she prefers. Or she may like a bronzed rather than a blushed look. I ask brides to provide images from wedding magazines, Pinterest, or online sources showing the esthetic they would like to achieve. It is important that we are on the same page. No artist wants to be at the completion of any makeup application only to discover that their client's expectations haven't been met.

Consider yet another perspective. A client is lying down, they give you absolutely no direction whatsoever, and you are told they shouldn't look better than they do on a very average day. My students who were also morticians confided with me about their unique daily challenges. In their funeral home jobs, they didn't have the opportunity to discuss a look with their clients. The families do not want their loved ones to appear different from usual.

These specialized students of mine also shared that the hands-on practice in our class was a bit awkward for them. They were accustomed to their models lying down and motionless, rather than active and sitting up straight. Talk about a different way of looking at things!

Could seeing things from a different angle or vantage point help you?

All Ears

There is a voice that doesn't use words. Listen.

Rumi Poet and theologian

When you have the privilege of doing makeup on someone, they will often volunteer their concerns. For example, "I need your help covering up the bags under my eyes," or, "I have this scar I am hoping you can conceal." It seems basic, but make sure that you address their requests along with those obvious to you. When a new SYFY actor stated to me on a photo shoot, "Please don't make me look orange," I figured he must have had a bad experience he did not want repeated. Those listening skills ultimately led to me being cast as key makeup artist on his network television show.

Hoping to chat it up with celebrities? Realize that makeup application is frequently their only time to relax, review their lines, or make a few calls. As crew, we speak, for the most part, only when spoken to. Remember, it is not all about you.

A famous and talented makeup artist once revealed in a seminar that when hiring her assistants, she looked for those who, "followed her direction, were good – not necessarily great – at doing makeup, and those who kept quiet." She, like others in the industry, understood the importance of being seen but not heard. Could talking less help your career?

Confidential

Most of us can keep a secret. It's the people we tell it to who can't.

Unknown

Most of my projects require confidentiality or non-disclosure agreements. That is the reason I do not name names in this book. It makes perfect sense. As their makeup artist, I do and see many things that the client prefers to keep private.

Perhaps unbeknownst to the public, they wear a toupee or a wig. Or they might request a product for building hair fibers to cover their balding scalp. Maybe their desire to look more youthful requires me to incorporate face lift tape during our session. Trimming nose hairs, covering scars, and hiding recent bruises are all part of the job!

I have worked at the private homes and offices of many celebrities, most of which have been very beautiful, but there have been a few trashy ones. I have even experienced a double request for secrecy. Though I had already signed a non-disclosure agreement (NDA) in advance for the project, upon approaching a celebrity's fancy Bel-Air home on the day of the shoot, I had to stop at a mini guard gate just a few feet from the house to sign five more pages of confidentiality restrictions. Wouldn't you just love to know who that was?

NDAs protect the stars from tabloid stories. Talent often discusses personal issues on set or make what they consider to be private comments or phone calls. Their children often accompany them on location. Imagine if something was leaked that impacted their career or their personal life.

Simply the belief that an artist had leaked a star's wedding details cost a high-profile makeup person his livelihood. When word got out about the celebrity's upcoming nuptials, for some reason, the makeup artist was targeted as the source despite being the star's longtime collaborator and friend. Not guilty of the indiscretion, he still lost his exclusive client and was very much shunned within the industry. Eventually he was able to rebuild his career, but only after much difficulty and heartache. While it did ultimately come out that he was innocent of all wrongdoing, the damage was done.

When work or friends request confidentiality, it is imperative that you respect their wishes. Can you keep a secret?

Manners

Politeness is to human nature what warmth is to wax.

Arthur Schopenhauer Philosopher

Are you well-mannered in your job and life? Never underestimate the power of the words *please* and *thank you*. They really can make a big difference in how you make others feel.

One of my very favorite celebrity clients is a director, a producer, and a composer. Having done his makeup many times, I have found him to be the most polite person I have ever met. Almost after each and every brush stroke, he thanks me. When the rest of the crew is simply doing their job, he praises them. Considering his incredible level of success, I wonder if along with his amazing talents, could it be this attitude of gratitude that has catapulted him to super stardom? I don't doubt it for a second.

I try to show the people that I work with my appreciation for the opportunities, for the food, and for their friendships. I aspire to be gentle and thoughtful with each of my clients and show concern about their needs. Is the pressure of my application just right? Do they have any special requests? Any allergies I should know about? It helps them to know that I care.

When greeting someone on set, I make eye contact, give a big smile, and shake their hand firmly. Hugs are not always welcomed, so it's best to ask first. Old school formal, I refer to clients by their title and last name unless they tell me otherwise. How do you act when meeting new people?

The Life

Less

Simplicity is the ultimate sophistication.

Leonardo da Vinci   Renaissance painter, sculptor, and inventor

Do you imagine that most clients want dramatic makeovers when they work with a professional artist? Surprisingly, that is not usually the case. "Like themselves on a good day" is how most people prefer to look after a makeup session. They don't want to appear as if they are wearing a heavy mask or are radically different from themselves.

As a makeup artist, I carefully choose products, colors, and techniques to accomplish this goal. For mature skin, this is even more critical since too much makeup or the wrong product can emphasize lines and textures that would best be minimized. Less is more has become my mantra.

If you are a makeup junkie, please enjoy some makeup-free days. Constant use of products can take a toll on one's face. Not just the application and daily wear, it can even be the removal. Waterproof mascara, anyone? I have personally seen clients in their thirties with scarring on eyelids from their daily wearing of false eyelashes. It is obviously just too much. Take gentle care of your skin and let it breathe anytime you can. Most people actually prefer their partners with less makeup.

I knew a woman whose family never, ever saw her without makeup. She wore her makeup to bed, washed it off in her morning shower, and would not come out of the bathroom until her face was once again made up. She most likely suffered from makeup addiction. Don't fall into this trap. Learn to love yourself without all the goodies. You are beautiful already.

Besides makeup breaks, I also recommend simplicity. Own fewer products of better quality that can multitask. Keep this in mind when building your kit. And beyond the makeup collection, this philosophy can also relate to your wardrobe and home decor. Buy multipurpose items or only accumulate those you truly cherish. Enjoy them judiciously. Isn't that a much healthier way of living for you and our Earth?

Vulnerability

What makes you vulnerable makes you beautiful.

Brené Brown   Author and professor

Could a makeup chair hold special powers? I believe so.

My director-style chair becomes magical as soon as a client sits down in it. The confessions begin. Newly-seated guests start to reveal what they perceive to be their flaws. A big nose, dark shadows under their eyes, pimples on their chin... the list goes on and on.

A 2016 TED Talk by Eva DeVirgilis (fellow makeup artist and actress) discusses this very real phenomenon. She shares our secret: we don't see you in the same way. Your makeup artist focuses instead on your beauty and potential, not your imperfections.

Perhaps clients share their perceived inadequacies so that we as technicians can repair them. Insecurities are inevitable, and a makeup application is an extremely intimate experience. Clients are simply sharing their vulnerabilities. I can relate; there is very good reason why I personally prefer to be behind, rather than in front of, the camera. Vulnerability is not easy.

Please, however, don't judge yourself simply by the mirror. It is hardly the whole picture. Your kindness, intelligence, sense of humor, and quirky style are far more interesting to others than the slight blemish you might see. Have you ever noticed how others are usually far more worried about how they look anyway?

Helping Others

Life's most urgent question is: 'What are you doing for others?'

Martin Luther King, Jr. Minister and social rights activist

"How can I help?" Four very powerful words. When starting my business, I realized quickly that I needed more practice as well as more contacts. Volunteering my time and talents helped with both.

I began assisting on student projects at local film schools. The first makeup credit I earned was on one of those films. That participation, along with other student projects, was instrumental in exposing me to the magical world of movie production.

Helping with the American Cancer Society's *Look Good, Feel Better* program was equally beneficial. I assisted women of all ages who were going through cancer treatments. Wigs, scarves, and makeup were my tools to bring back their sense of normalcy and beauty during this difficult life event. What a humbling experience.

Belle of the Ball is yet another wonderful opportunity to make a difference in the lives of others. At-risk and foster care teen girls are given brand new prom gowns, shoes, and accessories along with self-esteem classes. Artists donate their time by providing makeup lessons so that the girls can recreate their own beautiful looks on prom night.

Helping out isn't just about making faces pretty. *Every 15 Minutes* events are mock drunk driving scenarios usually staged around prom time at high schools. The goal is to help prevent alcohol-related accidents. We simulate extremely graphic injuries on a few students, which delivers a powerful message to their fellow classmates.

Recently, I was recruited by a local hospital to provide a realistic-looking active shooter scenario. Nursing students acted as the severely injured patients. A sad commentary on life today, yet these types of drills really do help first responders to better prepare both mentally and physically for these potential emergencies.

On a much lighter note, offering face painting for children has helped entertain the crowds of people attending my local *Race for the Rescue* events that promote the adoption of stray animals. Watching youngsters' faces light up when they see your creativity in the mirror is always joyful.

With each of these events, I received so much more than I gave. The smiles, appreciation, and lessons learned have enriched my life as an artist as well as a person. It feels so good to help others; it benefits the community.

Sharing your talents, whether they are in makeup artistry or any other field, by volunteering can be a game changer. Have you thought about how you might use your skills to help heal the world?

Impermanence

Thanks to impermanence, everything is possible.

Thich Nhat Hanh   Buddhist monk and peace activist

Have you ever heard Mark Twain's quote, "If you don't like the weather in New England now, just wait a few minutes"? Growing up in Boston, I found it to be true. Life itself can be similar to the climate back East. And a very good thing that is. One of the essential ideas in Buddhist philosophy is the concept of impermanence. All conditioned existence, without exception, is "transient, evanescent, and inconstant." Basically, things won't stay the same; there will always be change.

If your life is going swimmingly well, be sure to take the time to really enjoy it. Save some of that extra money. Share your joy with others. Success and happiness can and will change. On the other hand, if you are depressed or life is getting you down, find relief in the fact that "this too shall pass." Both ends of the spectrum are part of the human experience.

To help protect you and your livelihood, it's a good idea to have an alternative income stream or Plan B up your sleeve for when things shift. Diversify. If my freelance gigs are not as busy, I rely on my makeup classes as another revenue source. I have supplemented my skill repertoire by learning how to do hair bling, which brings more sparkle into the world and also a little more money to my pocket. And my bartending certification comes in handy occasionally too. "Would you like a margarita with your mascara?"

To support yourself and others encountering impermanence, compassion is essential. Know that even those who might appear to have it all can have or have had their personal crosses to bear. Everyone experiences difficulties. No one lives very long on this Earth without encountering hardships. When you have the choice to be anything, definitely be kind.

One never knows how or when the twists and turns in life will take place. But if you are always looking out for new opportunities and are empathetic, the storms might be just a bit easier to weather. Because, as in Boston, it will snow one day. Of that you can be certain. Are you ready for winter?

Sparkle

Don't let the insecurities of others dull your sparkle. Shine like the star you are born to be.

Karen Civil Entrepreneur

Want to bring more joy to your world? Add a bit of sparkle. Seriously, it works!

A few years ago, I learned the art of applying hair bling from another makeup artist. It's similar to adding tinsel to a Christmas tree, except these strands of iridescent colors are knotted at the roots of a client's hair. They can stay in for a few days or sometimes even weeks, and are absolutely lovely.

But don't just take my word for it. While traveling in Europe last year, my French customs agent was extremely serious during the inspection. He stared me up and down, kept looking at my passport, all without uttering a single word. I had nothing to declare, but was becoming more and more anxious anyway. After what seemed like an eternity, he finally confessed, "I can't stop looking at your hair," and proceeded to inquire all about it. He was in awe.

His reaction is not uncommon with hair bling. Women everywhere are extremely curious and ask how it is done when they see my hair bling. Men seem equally, if not more, interested. Somehow these tiny sparkling strands make both the wearer and the observer feel happy. It is definitely a conversation starter.

I learned of a similar phenomenon after meeting an actress with cotton candy pink hair. She confided to me that she felt as though she had magical powers because of her blush-toned locks. People could not stop staring. They loved it.

Regarding sparkle: according to the "rules," bridal makeup should have absolutely none of it. Instead, the look should be completely matte: no reflective products such as frosted shadows or pearl-like highlighters. If worn, the camera's flash could magnify the makeup's iridescence and overpower the client's features.

My personal experience, however, has taught me that if a bride wears glittery makeup every other day of her life, there is absolutely no way she would go without it on her wedding day. And as the paying client, she chooses exactly what she wants. And that seems to be glitter. Lots of glitter.

I worked as a production designer and makeup artist for a holiday photo shoot. Studio execs and their families were given the choice between two different backgrounds: the brilliant twinkly-lit one that I brought in, or the standard brown matte backdrop provided by the production company. Care to guess which one won? Yes, most holiday cards that year sparkled with lights. Hands down, it was my favorite and that of the participants. Sparkle usually wins.

I hope that you find your unique way to shine. It doesn't have to be with bling or cotton candy colored hair. You might discover another twinkle vehicle, such as makeup, clothing, jewelry, nails, shoes, or even your personality. Whatever works, but do share your sparkle.

Success

Success is liking yourself, liking what you do, and liking how you do it.

Maya Angelou   Poet, singer, and civil rights activist

I am blessed to have enjoyed many great moments in my career as a makeup artist: prepping on interviews for blockbuster movies, working as the key makeup artist on a SYFY television show, and meeting some of the biggest stars in Hollywood. This profession has exposed me to brilliant minds in a wide variety of fields, far beyond the film and television industry. And not for one second have I taken it for granted. But how might I determine if I have been successful?

My measures for achievement are eclectic. Here are some of them:

- **Phone calls received for new opportunities.** I never tire of getting calls for work. I really love my job!
- **Referrals from satisfied clients.** Word of mouth is good. That means they really liked your work.
- **Clients and crew who have become friends.** It's a treat to meet new people and to grow your friend circle. I recall blushing when a new co-worker said, "Nice working with you, Baby Girl."
- **Students who have gone on to secure even better jobs than mine.** Some of my former students have done magazine

covers, won theatre awards, and basically trumped my level of talent. Maybe one day I will be mentioned in an Academy Awards acceptance speech? I hope so.

- **Credits on IMDb and on screen after television shows, interviews, and movies.** Internet Movie Data Base (imdb.com) lists the crewmembers on specific industry projects. It feels super cool to be named on this Hollywood website. And the thrill of seeing Carolyn Simon, makeup artist, roll by on a screen is definitely priceless!

- **Selection as an expert witness for a legal case involving makeup.** It ended up being settled out of court, but it was quite a compliment just to be asked.

- **Brides who pass me along to their extended families to do makeup for wedding after wedding.** I have done four different weddings for one lovely group. I am starting to feel like part of their family.

- **Gaining the trust of Academy Award-winning makeup artists to do their makeup.** Nothing is quite as nerve-racking or more rewarding than doing makeup on one of your makeup idols.

- **Doing a photo shoot with Santa and Mrs. Claus.** Each day on set is an adventure. I never expected to work with the man in red and I honestly felt like a kid again.

- **Compliments from a "Sexiest Man Alive" about my signature scent.** My kind of job. Yes, he was pretty darn sexy!

- **Recognition from my dad (finally!) after doing makeup on big stars from Boston.** One always wants to make their parents proud, and working with two of Beantown's most famous actors did just that for me. And they were wicked nice to this Revere girl.

- **Feeling like I have never worked a day while earning a living as a makeup artist.** Don't tell anyone, but I would probably do makeup for free. Luckily, my clients want to be sure I can pay for food and shelter.

What are or will be your measures of success?

Finally...

For attractive lips, speak words of kindness. For lovely eyes, seek out the good in people. For a slim figure, share your food with the hungry. For beautiful hair, let a child run his or her fingers through it once a day. For poise, walk with the knowledge that you never walk alone.

Sam Levenson Author

Know that you are enough. Actually, you are more than enough. This business of makeup, of seeing pretty faces every day, has helped me to appreciate a more authentic type of beauty. Real, not reel, beauty.

Paints and powders, while they may provide a great visual esthetic, all too often become the masks behind which we hide. We become increasingly dependent on them to face the world.

As we build up tolerance, we may eventually seek out longer-wearing or more permanent solutions such as lash extensions, tattoos, fillers, and even surgery. It becomes a cat and mouse game that we will never win. And we are simply missing the point, because superficial or manufactured attractiveness inevitably fades.

Those who instead cultivate a meaningful life will always be radiant. The beauty of someone who appreciates each and every day, engages with others in loving kindness, continues to grow and learn, and has a purpose larger than themselves, has no limits.

Now you know my secrets for a pretty great life. Are you ready for yours?

Acknowledgements

Ultimately what makes a pretty great life is not the career, the money, or the fame. It is the amazing people who surround you.

Thank you to my wonderful siblings: Susan, Buddy, Denise, Patrick, Kevin, Daniel, and Joan. Sharing bedrooms, one bathroom, and my formative years with you taught me how to get along with different types of people. I learned so much from each and every one of you. I am forever grateful to have you in my life.

I would like to acknowledge a few of the glamorous women who have influenced my life. My aunt Betty was, to young me, an icon of feminine beauty from the exotic land of California. My very first boss, Denise, was also an inspiration. Although limited in mobility, she was larger than life. And my mother-in-law, Barbara, who epitomizes class and style.

Above all, my mom Evelyn. Though a mother of eight children, she always made an effort and looked lovely. A voracious reader, she would have finished this book in a heartbeat, in between watching *Law & Order* or her beloved Tom Brady on the field. I can feel her smiling down on me right now.

And to my dad, FXC, who I can picture reading this paperback from his blue chair in the living room. He probably would be dozing off between chapters, but whatever. He was the best dad a girl could ever ask for!

And speaking of family, I cannot forget my many nieces and nephews; it is so wonderful to watch you grow into the pretty strong, pretty funny, and pretty smart people that you are today. This book may interest many of you. More importantly though, I hope that I'm your favorite aunt wherever I live.

Much gratitude to my small but powerful book community. Writing opened my eyes to a whole new world and to friends I had never imagined – literary people! From Hamid who supported me from day one and introduced me to many of the resources that I grew to rely upon, to Gabi (word nerd extraordinaire) of the Los Angeles Writers Critique group who believed in my project and helped to refine my words. And thanks to the smaller, but sweet, Sierra Madre Writers group whose members include Kris, Geneva, Christine, Johanna, Toni, Tamir, Terry, and Rosemary. Each gave me helpful feedback during my writing process. I know that they share in my joy today.

Many longtime friends influenced me during the book development process. Janell was always ready to help, Richie provided his knowledge and sharp wit, and authors Sam and Leslee directed me toward the self-publishing path. Gratitude also to Florence, a non-makeup wearing girl who threw in her support when I needed it most. And to Ellen who believed in the concept from the early days and who helped with the initial design. Thank you all.

Dear girlfriends, I am so very blessed to have you in my life. Almost all of you have been models for makeup or hair bling at some point in time! Lynda, Penny, Deb*, Jane, Cheryl, Lori, MJ, Pam, Jackie, Nancy, Beth*, Ellen, Julie*, Suzanne, Susan, Maureen, Dorene, Patti, Janis, Kelly*, Constance, Kathleen, Eileen, etc., I wouldn't be here – or want to be – without each of you. (*means there's more than one with same name)

Thank you to Hay House and their self-publishing branch, Balboa Press. An avid self-help book reader, I knew that I was in the best possible company alongside Louise Hay, Dr. Wayne Dyer, and Kelly Notaras.

To my former students/readers, Timothy, Mai, and Dorene, I so appreciated your candid and constructive feedback. You were all super students and are even better people. Gratitude also to my brother,

Kevin. As a reader, he tends to look at things differently which was very helpful. And a huge THANK YOU to reader, Sonia, who is a very prominent person in this book and luckily in my life. I would not be the makeup artist I am, nor had any material to write, without her.

To all of my wonderful clients, fellow crew members, and especially former students, thank you from the bottom of my heart. This book reflects the lessons that I learned with and from you. I have enjoyed working alongside every one of you and look forward to sharing many more adventures together! I hope that you hear my voice as you are reading.

Merci to Terry for being a strong advocate of this project. He shared in my excitement, supported my vision, and is much appreciated.

Special thanks to my sister, Susan who has been unwavering in her willingness to listen to my whining when things have been tough, but also gladly sharing in so many good times with me. Thank you, SZQ.

Thank you to Russ, for giving me the emotional and financial support needed as I was starting my career in Hollywood and still today. But even more for giving me a priceless gift...

To Parker, my amazing son. I learn from you every single day and am so proud of the smart, funny, caring guy you have become. You are my light. I am forever grateful for you and for the many others who have helped me along this journey.

About the Author

Carolyn Simon is a curator of all things beautiful: faces, places, and experiences. As a Hollywood makeup artist/groomer, she works with the biggest studios and networks including ABC, Amazon, CBS, Netflix, Paramount Pictures, Walt Disney, and Warner Bros. She also teaches her craft to upcoming artists in makeup courses and workshops. And whenever possible, she can be found traveling to Europe, especially to France.

carolynsimonmakeup.com
Facebook: Carolyn Simon Makeup
Instagram: Carolyn Simon Makeup

Author photograph by Angel Padua

CPSIA information can be obtained
at www.ICGtesting.com
Printed in the USA
LVHW020415170322
713568LV00007B/780